Art Deco Fashion
Masterpieces

Publisher and Creative Director: Nick Wells
Project Editor: Polly Prior
Art Director: Mike Spender
Layout Design: Jane Ashley
Digital Design and Production: Chris Herbert

Special thanks to: Stephen Feather, Karen Fitzpatrick, Catherine Taylor and Laura Bulbeck

14 16 15 13
3 5 7 9 10 8 6 4 2

This edition first published 2012 by
FLAME TREE PUBLISHING
Crabtree Hall, Crabtree Lane
Fulham, London SW6 6TY
United Kingdom

www.flametreepublishing.com

© 2012 this edition Flame Tree Publishing Limited

ISBN 978-0-85775-376-2

Printed in China

Art Deco Fashion
Masterpieces

Gordon Kerr

FLAME TREE
PUBLISHING

Contents

Art Deco: The Machine Age

THE ART DECO STYLE FLOURISHED in the decorative arts, architecture and painting from the 1920s. Functional and modern, it was characterized by clean lines, stylized flower patterns and geometric forms, with designers exploiting the new machine technology and materials of the age, such as Bakelite. They also worked in a variety of other materials including aluminium, stainless steel, lacquer, inlaid wood and sharkskin.

Art Deco's sense of modernity was further enhanced by the inspiration it took from aspects of machine design: the workings of engines, the bow of a yacht or the shape of a luxury cruise-ship's porthole. The streamlined forms of radios, buildings and other objects were a visual metaphor for this fast-moving age.

Art Deco drew influences from a variety of sources and was a highly eclectic style; the writer F. Scott Fitzgerald (1896–1940) claimed that this came from 'all the nervous energy stored up and expended in the War'.

Parisian design, showcased at the 1925 Paris Exposition, was pre-eminent and its influence in almost every sphere of the arts was inestimable. During the 1920s, for the first time, the great couturiers of Paris brought fashion design to the fore, making it as influential as any other design medium. Soon, it had become a vivid expression of the new attitudes and morality being enthusiastically embraced by forward-thinking people in the aftermath of the Great War.

Origins

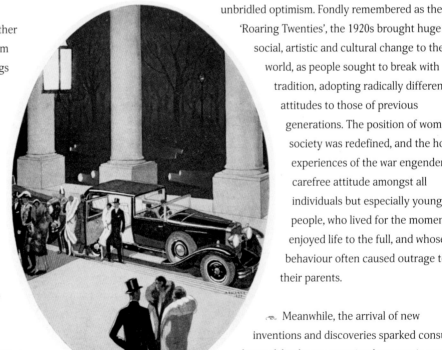

The First World War was followed by a period of unbridled optimism. Fondly remembered as the 'Roaring Twenties', the 1920s brought huge social, artistic and cultural change to the world, as people sought to break with tradition, adopting radically different attitudes to those of previous generations. The position of women in society was redefined, and the horrific experiences of the war engendered a carefree attitude amongst all individuals but especially young people, who lived for the moment and enjoyed life to the full, and whose behaviour often caused outrage to their parents.

Meanwhile, the arrival of new inventions and discoveries sparked consumer demand, leading to sustained economic growth and prosperity.

Roaring Twenties

The epithet the 'Roaring Twenties' was coined to describe the dynamic, innovative and iconoclastic years of the 1920s. Following the horrors of the First World War, this decade of growth brought huge social, artistic and cultural change to the world with the arrival of new gadgets, materials, attitudes and morals.

The position of women in society, having already undergone necessary adjustment during the war years, changed radically, while the arrival of new inventions and discoveries changed the lives and aspirations of ordinary people for ever. It was the decade of jazz music and dance crazes, but it was also the decade of the eclectic artistic and design movement Art Deco, whose influence would go on to colonize every area of artistic endeavour.

The Roaring Twenties signalled a break with pre-war traditions and a conscious pursuit of modernity. This was often expressed through modern technology which, following the privations endured during the war, seemed to make everything possible. Radio, motorcars and moving pictures symbolized this notion of modernity, as practicality superseded the decorative formality that had been prevalent before the war. Of course, the decade would end with the catastrophic stock market crash of 1929, but the nine or so years before that saw economies growing vigorously, industry moving into mass production and people becoming avid consumers of the goods being produced.

The Roaring Twenties were experienced across the world – in France and Francophone Canada, they were known as 'Les Années Folles' – but it was in the United States that the greatest social and cultural impacts were felt. Three consecutive Republican administrations contributed to this, with reductions in the punitive taxes of the war years made by President Warren Harding (1865–1923) resulting in a boom during the tenure of his successor, Calvin Coolidge (1872–1933). Therefore, consumer spending on mass-produced technology that the middle classes could now afford increased. The automobile industry, in particular, rocketed during the 1920s, with cars being produced in huge quantities throughout the United States and Canada. The Model T Ford was discontinued in 1927, but only after 15 million had been sold.

People's lives and leisure time were radically altered by the new medium of radio. Radio sets remained expensive but there were enough of them in use to attract advertising and marketing, and further develop the communications industry that has dominated our lives ever since.

Meanwhile, vaudeville and music hall as forms of entertainment for the masses began to pall in comparison to the Hollywood movie stars that glittered on the screens of the world's cinemas. When the miracle of sound was added to films in 1927, their grip on the world's imagination tightened; to go to the cinema was cheap and easy, and people turned up in their droves to worship the gods of the silver screen.

For women, life changed immeasurably. Unmarried women were increasingly employed in clerical jobs, and their new role in this decade was symbolized by their new political equality. In August 1920, Tennessee was the last state of the Union to ratify the Nineteenth Amendment, finally giving American women the right to vote, while in Britain the Representation of the People Act of 1918 enfranchised women over the age of 30 who were either a member or married to a member of the Local Government Register.

One way in which women expressed this changing role was in the clothes they wore, and in the 1920s, fashion became a social statement as well as a trend or simply a way of looking good. It represented a complete break with the rigidities imposed upon people during Victorian times. The new breed of young women who espoused this new look and attitude were known by their elders, somewhat disparagingly, as 'flappers'.

The 'Golden Twenties', as this period was also known, were brought to an abrupt halt in 1929. In 1921, the Dow Jones Industrial Average had stood at a value of 63.9. By September 1929, on the back of the technological advances of the decade and an overweening confidence in the markets, it had increased six-fold, sitting at 381.2. By 11 November, however, the bubble had burst and it had dropped by 40 per cent, finally bottoming out in July 1932. By then, the brash, exciting Roaring Twenties, when everything had seemed possible, were little more than a distant memory.

Paris Exposition 1925

The important Exposition Internationale des Arts Décoratifs et Industriels Modernes of 1925 aimed to restore French decorative arts, fashion and luxury goods to the forefront of international design in the face of growing international competition. It intended to do so by blending French expertise and taste in the design of luxury goods with the opportunities provided by the technologies of modern mass production.

Producers of luxury goods and glass designers such as René Lalique (1860–1945) were prominent, and the French section of the exhibition occupied about two-thirds of the 57-acre site. Many of the most exciting displays of the entire exhibition were created by the Société des Artistes Décorateurs. Their 'Reception Rooms and Private Apartments of a French Embassy' occupied 25 fully furnished rooms that surrounded a three-sided courtyard. Elements of these designs would go on to influence Hollywood film sets, cinema foyers, restaurants, ocean liner interiors and corporate foyers.

Fashion had a major presence at the exhibition, with the designs of leading French couturiers such as The House of Jenny, Charles Worth (1826–95, *see left and also page 77*) and Jeanne Lanvin (1867–1946) being shown in the Pavillon de l'Élégance. Meanwhile, three large barges moored on the Seine carried displays of Paul Poiret's (1879–1944) work, whereas Sonia Delaunay's (1885–1979) clothing and textiles could be seen in the Boutique Simultané.

By the time the Paris Expo closed in October 1925, more than 16 million people had passed through its doors. Its influence was immediately felt across the industrialized world and the Art Deco style that it epitomized began to shape design everywhere.

The Jazz Age

F. Scott Fitzgerald, author of *The Great Gatsby*, coined the phrase 'the Jazz Age' to describe the 'anything goes' era that emerged in the United States after the First World War; a decade that represented a hedonistic and, some would say, cynical interlude between the Great War and the Great Depression. It was a period during which young people, whose belief in the morality and social conventions of their elders had perhaps been destroyed by the horrors of the war, rebelled and participated in a frenzy of consumption and speculation.

Jazz, along with (to a lesser extent) ragtime and blues, all originating from the African-American community, provided the soundtrack to this decade, and its most famous exponents became Louis Armstrong (1901–71), Fats Waller (1904–43) and Benny Goodman (1909–86). This music engendered new, provocative dances such as the Charleston, the Black Bottom, the Cubanola Glide and the Tango Argentino, which outraged many. Animal dances – the Kangaroo Hop, the Turkey Trot and the Bunny Hug – became popular for a time.

The jazz lifestyle was appealing to a lot of young white girls and boys, many of whom used it to escape from the drudgery of rural America. But the new music was blamed for everything, from drunkenness to deafness and an increase in unmarried mothers. In small towns throughout the land, however, jazz bands played the new music and if a band was not readily available, there was always the phonograph. 78 rpm records were cheaply available to everyone and jazz concerts featured on the new medium of the radio.

It was the era of 'flappers' or 'jazz babies': young women who, because of their clothes and attitudes, were looked upon with horror by the older generation. It was also the time of Prohibition, during which, even though outlawed, the sale and consumption of alcohol carried on unabated in speakeasies that echoed to the sounds of the new music, earning fortunes for gangsters such as Al Capone.

A Golden Age?

It seemed like a fresh start for the world. The 'war to end all wars' was deemed to have drawn a line under the past and optimism reigned. Freed from the restrictions of the Victorian and Edwardian ages, people wanted to create a new world in which they could enjoy life; as the war had proved, after all, life could be short. Industrial and technological advances provided the machines and devices that enhanced existence, and mass production made everything from radio sets to fashion items affordable and accessible to all. Everyone could participate in this streamlined and brightly coloured modern world.

Modernity

Everything, from biology to painting, it seemed, was being approached in a fresh and even revolutionary way. In painting, for instance, Georges Braque (1882–1963) and Pablo Picasso (1881–1973) invented Cubism, which provided a new way of perceiving the world, by analysing and fragmenting the objects and people depicted in their work and looking at them from many angles at the same time. This approach, revolutionary in nature,

contradicted the attitude of previous generations who espoused an evolutionary approach to most things. Young people in the 1920s placed greater emphasis on the present and the future than on the past, always looking forward to the next thing.

Visually, modernity was expressed in several ways during the Jazz Age. It was an age of bright, jewel colours. Fashion and fashion illustration glowed with swathes of vivid colour, as is evident from *Summer* (from *Falbalas & Fanfreluches*, 1925) (*see page 101*). Paintings, too, dazzled the viewer with their bright colours, as exhibited by Tamara de Lempicka's (1898–1990) 1929 painting, *Saint Moritz* (*see page* 128).

The fast pace of modern life was summed up by the new passion for streamlining, which often included things that did not even move. Aerodynamic shapes were expressed in fluid curves and long, straight, horizontal lines. It was as if speed itself were being depicted on buildings, radios, ocean-going liners and other objects.

The fad for modernity, for the latest invention, the latest fashion or the latest example of outrageous behaviour would be brought to a halt by the reality of events at the end of the decade – the financial crisis, the end of prosperity and the rise of the political extremism that led to the Second World War.

Technology

The 1920s were host to an astonishing array of technological advances that impacted the way people lived, worked and spent their leisure time.

A radio craze swept the world and especially America where, by 1923, 600 commercial radio stations had been set up and where, by 1930, 60 per cent of households had purchased radio sets on which they listened to broadcasts of music, sports and live events.

There was an explosion in cinema attendance in the 1920s, especially after the arrival of the 'talkies' in 1927 with *The Jazz*

Singer – the film that signalled the beginning of Hollywood's golden age.

Aviation dramatically altered travel, as aeroplanes began to be used in other ways than merely as weapons in warfare. Their use in delivering mail provided some much-needed impetus and Charles Lindbergh's (1902–74) 1927 solo, nonstop flight across the Atlantic opened people's eyes to even greater possibilities.

There were many other advances: Scottish inventor John Logie Baird (1888–1946) devised the first working mechanical television system in 1925; record companies introduced an electrical recording process in 1925 that gave phonograph records a more lifelike sound; American physicist Robert Goddard (1882–1945) carried out the first test flight of a liquid-fuelled rocket in 1926; and, in 1925, Clarence Birdseye (1886–1956) invented a process for freezing food. The hairdryer, antibiotics, the hearing aid, the electric razor, sticking

plasters and quartz timekeeping also first saw the light of day in the 1920s.

Luxury and Leisure

It did not take very long after the war for the social elite to return to its pre-war pastimes of hunting, racing, partying and holidaying abroad. By the winter of 1919, numerous shoots had been arranged and yachts that had remained in port for the duration of the war were undergoing refits. Well-to-do British people and wealthy Americans booked tickets on trains heading for the French Riviera, where they would spend the cold winter months (*see page* 117).

In London, nightclubs threw open their doors for the first time. Drugs – cocaine, heroin and opium – were being consumed by those who could afford them and theatre audiences attending

Noël Coward's (1899–1973) play, *The Vortex*, were shocked to find that drugs were a major theme of the play.

༧ Dancing became a craze as new rhythms arrived from America and even the Prince of Wales could be seen practising his steps. After the rigours of a week's hard partying, weekends would be spent relaxing in the country – shooting and fishing, or playing golf, tennis or croquet.

Illustration

༧ It was a golden age for illustration: a time of unprecedented brilliance and innovation in magazine and book illustration (*see page* 102). Advances in technology enabled accurate and inexpensive reproduction of pictures, and this was combined with a voracious public demand for new graphic art. There were also a large number of new magazines on the market, providing ample scope for illustrators to earn a living.

༧ Advertising became a major source of revenue for magazines and newspapers, and it provided fresh opportunities for artists to demonstrate their talents. It also challenged them with working in fresh, contemporary styles that complemented the Jazz Age as well as the other changes that were occurring in contemporary culture.

༧ In fashion, photography was still fairly rare and illustrations in the magazines promoting the designs of the great couturiers of the time were created by a generation of brilliantly talented illustrators who showed models in real-life situations, such as enjoying themselves at parties or at the seaside (*see page* 123).

Lifestyle

༧ The impact of the new methods of mechanization and mass production techniques was immense. Cars, radios and electrical products were produced more quickly and cost-effectively than ever before, and producers were able to sell them to people at prices they could afford. Labour-saving devices and new means of entertainment were available to all and life was radically changed by them.

༧ Cars were more affordable, providing opportunities for people to travel far greater distances than ever before. The availability

of personal transport also meant that workers did not have to live close to their place of employment and were freed from a reliance on public transport to get them to work. They could live, therefore, away from urban centres, in more rural environments on the outskirts of cities. Car sales had a crucial impact on infrastructure and employment: workers were needed to build the new roads required by the growth in motor travel and jobs became available in motels, service stations and car dealerships.

- Life became increasingly urbanized. In the United States and Canada, for the first time, more people lived in cities and towns than in rural areas. The major conurbations grew, and great monuments to the age and the prevailing Art Deco style were built, such as the Chrysler skyscraper in New York, which was constructed in 1928 (*see page* 121). In cities, it was not just the males of the family who found employment, but women, too, found increasing job opportunities as shop assistants, typists and filing clerks. These were relatively low-paid but for the first

time it meant that women had a degree of independence and they helped to bring in some much-needed extra income.

- Relationships changed. The motorcar impacted on the way that people courted in the 1920s. Previously, courting had been a rather restrained affair, carried out according to the strictures of the Victorian moral code, in full view of the parents of the young couple involved. Nothing inappropriate was permitted and the pair were forbidden from any form of physical contact. The motorcar changed that. Suddenly, young, amorous couples had the means to get far away from prying and disapproving eyes, and the car provided all the privacy they needed. The concept of dating was born. If a car was not available, however, there were other options – restaurants, speakeasies, the ever-popular dance halls and the dark back rows of cinemas. The new morality meant that premarital and extramarital sex became more common than before, as revealed by a 1928 survey showing that 25 per cent of all married American men and women confessed to at least one adulterous affair.

- Even within marriage, however, great changes occurred during the 1920s. In Victorian times, men and women moved in separate spheres, where men socialized with other men and women with other women. In the 1920s, though, couples began to do things together, sharing activities and often socializing with other like-minded couples.

- The more relaxed attitude to sex contributed greatly to this change. It was still illegal to distribute or use birth control devices in many areas of the United States, but increasing numbers of women were using them. Birth control activist Margaret Sanger (1879–1966) imported the diaphragm illegally from Germany and Holland from 1916 onwards and helped fund the first American manufacturer of them in 1925. Sales of condoms rocketed in the 1920s, although they were always referred to euphemistically as items of 'feminine hygiene'. Women began to find that, freed from the fear of having another child, they could enjoy sex. It was no longer an obligation, but something to be enjoyed.

Art - Goût - Beauté

Nowadays, we take sport for granted and, as well as providing exercise for many, it is also one of the most popular forms of entertainment. This had not been the case before the First World War, but the 1920s changed that. Sports and sports stars started to enjoy huge publicity and promoters began to understand that a great deal of money could be made from events that up until that time had been largely amateurish.

In America, a professional football league was formed, golf tours were established and the tennis circuit was organized. These drew large crowds of fans hungry to see the stars they worshipped, many of whom are still known today, such as Babe Ruth (1895–1948) in baseball, Jack Dempsey (1895–1983) in boxing, Bill Tilden (1893–1953) and Helen Wills (1905–98) in tennis, Bobby Jones (1902–71) in golf and Red Grange (1903–91) in American football.

Influences

Art Deco was an eclectic style that took its influences from a range of sources, but was also affected by the developments and new opportunities of the time, such as foreign travel.

It was a period of exploration of the past through archaeological excavation, and the discoveries of artefacts from distant and exotic times inspired artists and designers, who incorporated concepts and motifs from those discoveries

into their work, whether it was architecture, jewellery or fashion design. Elements were borrowed from ancient historical styles, such as Greco-Roman Classicism and Babylonian, Assyrian, Ancient Egyptian, Aztec and African art (*see below and also page 98*).

The modern world also wielded an influence over Art Deco practitioners. They borrowed motifs of the machine age to showcase in their work, such as the technique of streamlining. Radio, aviation, electric lighting, ocean liners and skyscrapers also provided inspiration.

Art Deco was also significantly influenced by the other art and design movements that preceded and developed alongside it: Art Nouveau, Cubism, Russian Constructivism and Italian Futurism.

Art Nouveau

⮞ Like Art Deco, Art Nouveau sprang out of a major world event: the Industrial Revolution. Emerging around 1880 in Europe, it was a reaction to the realism of the academic art of the nineteenth century and found expression in architecture and applied art – especially the decorative arts. Its practitioners embraced Europe's new industrial aesthetic, and their work featured sinuous, stylized forms and structures which often combined swirling geometric shapes and plants and flowers.

⮞ Art Deco, with its simpler, less cluttered approach to design, was considered for a long time to be the direct opposite of Art Nouveau. Nowadays, however, the belief is that it was more of an extension of its predecessor, especially in its preoccupation with lavish and luxurious design, its use of fine materials and its expression by extraordinarily gifted craftsmen.

⮞ Crucially, Art Nouveau also launched the process of blurring the distinctions between art, architecture and the applied arts – a process that was embraced and completed by Art Deco.

Aztec and Egypt

⮞ The discovery by Howard Carter (1874–1939) of the tomb of the Ancient Egyptian boy king Tutankhamun, in November 1922, sparked a sudden explosion of interest in all things Egyptian. Egyptian images and motifs immediately became popular and lotus flowers, scarabs, hieroglyphics and pyramids were soon being used in jewellery, furniture, graphic design and architecture.

⮞ Egyptian architects had decorated their buildings with symbols, and Art Deco architects did the same. For instance, William Van Alen's (1883–1954) Chrysler Building in New York, built in 1928, is adorned with eagle hood ornaments, hubcaps and abstract images of cars.

⮞ Even fashion fell victim to the Egyptian fad, as shown by the 'Mummy Wrap' dress – evoking the layered bindings of an Egyptian mummy – that became one of the most popular dress designs of the 1920s.

⮞ Meanwhile, Aztec symbols appeared in countless jewellery designs, and architects working in the Art Deco style took inspiration from Aztec temples; New York's Empire State Building, for instance, with its tiered or stepped design and the ziggurat – terraced pyramid – also became a popular motif of the Art Deco style.

Futurism and Cubism

⮞ Like Art Deco, Cubism and Futurism were a reaction primarily against Impressionism, but also against Revivalism. In Cubism, pioneered as an art style by Pablo Picasso and Georges Braque, a break was made from the tradition of depicting things from a single viewpoint – in Cubist works, objects are built up from multiple angular facets. Cubist-inspired decoration can be seen on Art Deco upholstery, fabrics, wood veneers and in the details of many buildings designed in the Art Deco style.

⮞ Futurism was its Italian cousin but preoccupied itself with concepts of the future, such as speed, technology, youth and violence, as well as modern objects such as the car, the plane and the industrial city; many of these were also prominent in the thinking and work of Art Deco practitioners.

Decorative Art Form

Unlike many other parts of the world, where such a distinction did not apply, in post-Renaissance Europe, the decorative arts had become completely separated from fine arts. In Islamic art, for instance, the most prized works of art are of a decorative kind, whereas decorative arts in Europe are considered to be those concerned with the design and decoration of objects that are, in the main, valued for their utility rather than for their purely aesthetic qualities. This would imply that Art Deco was appreciated simply because it looked 'pretty', but this is far from the case. It did indeed look pretty, and it may not have been created from a deep aesthetic philosophy, but its value lay in what it brought to the spirit of an age and it has to be conceded that, visually, there are few eras that evoke such vivid imagery as the Art Deco era of the 1920s.

Changing Population

Few historical events can have been as traumatic and transformative as the First World War. A generation of young men was erased in the horror of the trenches and the sheer scale of the conflict meant that the effects of war were felt for the first time not just on the battlefield, but also on the domestic front, where women increasingly took on responsible roles outside the home. As a result, nothing would ever be the same again.

Women in the 1920s

Since so many men were sent across the Channel to fight, women, until then viewed primarily as housewives, were called upon to replace them in order to keep the country going. The struggle for women's rights – especially the vote – had further empowered women, opening their eyes to greater possibilities.

The pace of change was rapid. In August 1920, all women in the United States were finally given the vote and increasingly they began to appear in the workforce, often in clerical roles, although usually for minimal wages. In Britain, the Matrimonial Causes Act of 1923 meant that, in divorce, women were treated as the equals of men; wives could now divorce their husbands for adultery.

The invention of the electric self-starter for the motorcar led to another advance for women: since cars no longer had to be hand-cranked, they could drive without first seeking the assistance of a male.

In relationships too, much changed, as women in the 1920s became sexual beings. This development was helped by advances in birth control which, in marriage, reduced the number of children a woman bore, freeing her to live a life of her own and perhaps even manage a job as well as a home.

Liberalism

Ironically, in terms of what was to follow (Nazi Germany and Fascist Italy), the 1920s were a period of liberalism, possibly

born out of the need to free the world of the Victorian ethics and values that had led to war. Progressivism, as liberalism was often called, had a strong presence in the lives of women and the youth of the time; unsurprisingly, given the disaster of the previous few years, there were rallying cries for world peace, as well as support for such things as good governance, maternal care, better education and improved public health.

꙰ American ideas of what the modern world should be like began to influence Europe, but the economic turmoil of 1929 quickly brought an end to such notions.

Rejection of Victorian Era Values

꙰ It is not unusual for one generation to reject the morality and traditions of the generation immediately preceding it. In the case of the 1920s, however, the revolution in morality and behaviour can be ascribed to several factors.

꙰ The First World War had unleashed unimaginable horrors that led many to question the type of moral standards that had allowed it to happen. Victorian values encapsulated a strict code of social conduct in which everyone knew his or her place in society. Crime or risqué behaviour had no place in the rigid Victorian social edifice, and restraint was advocated in relationships and sexual matters.

꙰ In the aftermath of the carnage of the Great War, such niceties appeared trivial and even hypocritical. Furthermore, the loss of so many lives at such an early age was a constant reminder to the young people of the time of their own mortality. If they were also going to die young, they were determined to live as full and exciting a life as possible and that necessitated the abandonment of many of the values of the previous generation.

Mass Media

꙰ The concept of 'mass media' first emerged in the 1920s. Advances in the technology of such things as printing, radio, record pressing and film duplication finally made it affordable and possible to reach a large group of people with a message. This had never been achieved before, especially not so quickly and across such a wide geographical expanse; it meant that advertising and promotional messages, as well as cultural trends and fashions, could be spread to large numbers of people almost at the same time. Furthermore, showing a film, for instance, within a short space of time across America could unify the country in a shared cultural experience that managed to bring together a geographically, socially and economically disparate society as never before.

꙰ Without the exploitation of mass media communication, there is little doubt that the Roaring Twenties would not have roared quite so loudly.

Designers and Illustrators

IN THE 1920S, TWO FEROCIOUSLY talented worlds coincided with each other in one place when the world of the fashion designer and the world of the artist/illustrator met and worked together in Paris. Complementing each other in an unprecedented way, these fabulous artists and couturiers elevated fashion to the heights of fine art, capturing the artistic spirit of the age in their designs and the illustrations that presented them to the world.

The Media

- The term 'the media' was first used in the 1920s to describe the variety of ways of communicating directly with people. Before that, the medium of print was the primary means of transmitting information, news or advertising messages, but in the 1920s, radio, cinema and a huge variety of magazines catering for every kind of taste were now available and affordable, transforming the world for ever.

Magazines

- During the 1920s, magazines became extraordinarily popular and many new publications appeared on the market. *Time* magazine – a weekly digest of general news for men and women with no time on their hands – was first published in March 1923, while *Reader's Digest* – a condensation of articles about news and entertainment drawn from other magazines –

first hit the newsstands in 1922. Both these publications proved phenomenally successful and remain in print to this day.

- The remarkable explosion of interest in the movies and movie stars at the time led to the publication of numerous titles that celebrated Hollywood, such as *Screenland* and *Screen Play*, while other new publications such as *True Story*, with a circulation of 2 million, appealed to the more prurient side of human nature.

- At the same time, there was a fascination for fashion and style magazines that made the latest exotic Paris fashions available to everyone. These magazines were themselves fine examples of the Art Deco design style of the times, often using the vibrantly coloured technique of *pochoir* (*see pages 68–69*).

- Lucien Vogel's (1886–1954) high-society fashion magazine *Gazette du Bon Ton*, published between 1912 and 1925, aimed to establish fashion as art, as expressed by its first editorial claiming that 'the clothing of a woman is a pleasure for the eye that cannot be judged inferior to the other arts'. And, indeed, it featured many of the great illustrators and Art Deco artists of the time, including Georges Barbier (1882–1932), Erté (1892–1990) and Paul Iribe (1883–1935), who depicted models in various real, if often exotic, situations, such as Georges

Barbier's 'Leaving for the Casino' (*see above*). It also had exclusive contracts with a number of the main fashion houses, including Poiret, Redfern and Worth (*see pages* 42–43).

🖎 *Art, Goût Beauté* was inspired by *Gazette du Bon Ton* and demonstrates how important the oxygen of publicity was to designers then. Sponsored by the French textile firm Albert Godde, Bedin and Co., it provided an intimate, comprehensive and exquisitely illustrated picture of contemporary Parisian fashion. It was published 10 to 12 times a year in French, English and Spanish. Its matchless elegance and illustrative brilliance can be seen in 'Skating Elegance' (*see page* 78).

🖎 Other de luxe French fashion magazines included *Femina* (*see page* 97), *Le Jardin des Dames et des Modes* and *Comoedia Illustré*. Lucien Vogel also published *Les Feuillets d'Art*: a lavishly illustrated art magazine that demonstrated how close the artists of the fashion magazines had come to the world of art, by featuring fashion plates alongside work by some of the great artists of the day. *Modes et Manières d'Aujourd'hui* contained fashion plates lovingly executed by illustrators such as Georges Barbier, Robert Bonfils (1886–1972), Georges Lepape (1887–1971) and André Edouard Marty (1882–1974).

🖎 *Vogue* and *Vanity Fair* are two magazines that still exert a powerful influence over the style, fashion and mores of today and both are part of the publishing empire launched by Condé Montrose Nast (1873–1942) in the first decade of the twentieth century. In the 1920s, *Vogue* brought Paris fashion to the women of America through its detailed presentation of the latest styles, providing clothing patterns and designs – including adaptations for those of limited income – as well as ordering systems. *Vogue* made the new flapper style accessible to all.

🖎 Condé Nast began publishing *Dress and Vanity Fair* in 1913, but decided to rename it simply *Vanity Fair* a year later. In the 1920s, led by managing editor Robert Benchley (1889–1945) and boasting the best writers of the day, it became a chronicler of literature, the arts, sports, politics, cinema and high society, reflecting the fashions and behaviour of the age.

LE POUF
ROBE DU SOIR, DE PAUL POIRET
Nº 7 de la *Gazette*. Année 1924 Planche 58
Modèle déposé. Reproduction interdite.

Another magazine that is still published today is *Harper's Bazaar*. Founded in 1867, it was America's first fashion magazine and amongst its regular contributors some decades later was leading French couturier Paul Poiret, who penned pieces on fashion, promoting his own work and that of other Parisian designers, while encouraging American women to be more daring in the way they dressed.

The Silver Screen

In the United States, 100 million people went to see a movie every week during the Jazz Age, and Hollywood, whose population had risen from 35,000 in 1919 to 130,000 by 1925, became home to stars such as slapstick comics Charlie Chaplin (1889–1977), John Gilbert (1897–1936) and Douglas Fairbanks (1883–1939), as well as actresses such as Clara Bow (1905–65) and Mary Pickford (1892–1979). About 800 films were produced every year in the 1920s and movies were, indeed, big business, with a capital investment of more than $2 billion.

For the first seven years of the decade, films were silent, but they were becoming increasingly ambitious and extravagant, with the most popular genres being swashbucklers, historical extravaganzas and melodramas. It was also the era of great comedy, with Charlie Chaplin, Buster Keaton (1895–1966) and Harold Lloyd (1893–1971) making people roll in the aisles. Stars worked in what became known as the studio system, in which actors and directors were tied to a studio by long-term contracts. Studios built luxurious 'picture palaces' large enough for entire orchestras to accompany the action on the screen and at the start of the decade there were 20,000 cinemas in the United States.

In the 1927 film *The Jazz Singer*, its star Al Jolson (1886–1950) astonished audiences by introducing a song with the words, 'Wait a minute! Wait a minute! You ain't heard nothin' yet.' Those words signalled the arrival of the first 'talkie' and the end of the age of the silent film – and of the careers of many of the great stars of the Twenties.

The Designers

It took a group of extraordinarily talented and innovative people to change the way that women dressed in the 1920s and beyond, freeing them from the cumbersome and restrictive clothing of the past and reflecting the new political and personal freedoms being experienced by women in society.

They were inescapably linked to Art Deco, the prevailing artistic and decorative style of the day. Also, for the first time, the arts and fashion became inextricably connected, displaying a bond brilliantly expressed by the leading couturiers of the age.

Coco Chanel (1883–1971)

Fashion in the 1920s is said to have been invented on a cool day in Deauville, France, when Coco Chanel – perhaps the greatest of all French couturiers – threw on a man's large, black sweater and tied it low on the waist with a large handkerchief. Chanel claimed that everyone she met asked her

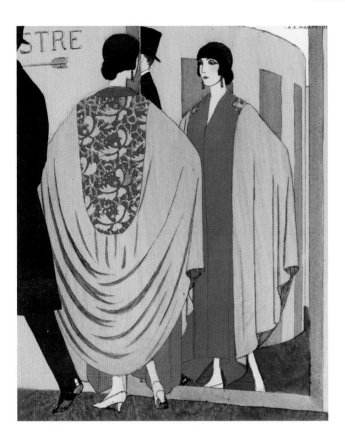

first to bear a designer's name. She designed costumes for the Ballets Russes and for Jean Cocteau's (1889–1963) play *Orphée* (1926), and long after her death, her fashion house continues at the forefront of fashion.

Callot Soeurs

The exclusive clothes designed by the four Callot sisters – Marie, Marthe, Regina and Joséphine – were prized for their exotic detail, as in their Design for an Evening Dress for a Reception on a Yacht in Cannes, 1928 (*see page* 125), and were very popular with actresses and international hostesses. The Callot Soeurs created the 'manteau d'abbé': the short cape flying from the shoulders of coats and evening gowns. They worked with unusual materials and were amongst the first designers to use lamé (a type of fabric woven with thin ribbons of metallic yarn or threads) in their designs. Silver and gold lamé dresses became very popular in the 1920s.

where she had bought the dress and by the time she returned to her shop she had sold ten.

Also one of the first women to wear trousers, cut her hair short and abandon the corset, the silhouette of Coco Chanel's clothing designs came to epitomize 1920s fashion and represented the look to which every woman aspired: the flapper look. She worked in neutral tones of beige, sand, cream, navy and black, and made her clothes from beautifully soft and fluid jersey fabrics cut with simple shapes that allowed the wearer to abandon restrictive corsetry and forget about the definition of the waist, so important to previous generations.

She designed revolutionary clothes that were all about comfort and ease of movement, as well as elegance. In the 1920s, she introduced many classic designs, including the iconic Chanel suit, the 'little black dress' and the perfume Chanel No. 5 – the

LA VISITE

ROSES ET MANTEAUX, DE JEANNE LANVIN

Modèles déposés. Reproduction interdite.

Année 1924-1925.

Jeanne Lanvin (1867–1946)

Lanvin designed the simple chemise dress that became the basic outline for the 1920s. Her trademarks were her skilful use of embroidery, sometimes with Aztec decoration ('The Visit' from the *Gazette du Bon Ton*, 1925, *see left*), and her exquisite craftsmanship. Her clothes were feminine, often decorated with ribbons, ruffles, flowers and lace that helped to create a 'young girl' look.

Paul Poiret (1879–1944)

Poiret, who made his name before the First World War, was one of the great couturiers and the first fashion designer to embrace the Art Deco style. Although influenced by numerous sources, it was the simplicity of Eastern garments and Eastern cutting techniques that helped him lay the foundations of twentieth-century fashion (*see page* 41).

Madame Tirocchi (1875–1947)

From her shop in Providence, Rhode Island, Anna Tirocchi provided her wealthy clients with the most beautiful French fabrics, purchased during her frequent visits to Europe. She sold custom-made dresses, or ready-to-wear, that used designs by Madame Agnes, Callot Soeurs, Jeanne Lanvin (*see page* 71), Paul Poiret and others.

Madeleine Vionnet (1876–1975)

Vionnet is perhaps best known for her Grecian-style dresses and for the introduction of the bias cut, which became her trademark and allowed her clothes to hang more gracefully or cling more, if narrow. Her designs were based on rigid geometric shapes and organic structures, leading to them often being compared to Cubist sculpture, as in the afternoon dress pictured in Souvenir de Pâques a Rome, *Gazette du Bon Ton*; No. 5, 1922 (*see below*).

Jean Patou (1887–1936)

Patou, who was responsible for the first designer label – identified by a 'J' and a 'P' on his pockets – became famous in the 1920s for his sportswear, especially the daring styles he designed for French tennis star Suzanne Lenglen (1899–1938). In 1925, he opened Sports Corner, a shop with different rooms for different sporting activities, where the clothes co-ordinated with accessories. In December 1924, he famously brought six American models to Paris because their leggy, lean physique was what he required in order to be able to sell his clothes to American women (*see right*).

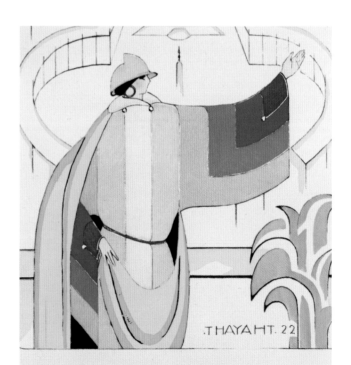

.THAYA HT. 22

SOUVENIR DE PAQUES A ROME

Elsa Schiaparelli (1890–1973)

One of the most prominent figures in fashion between the wars, along with Coco Chanel, Schiaparelli became known for her black knit sweaters with a white bow-tie pattern, as well as for her flair for the unusual. She was the first designer to use shoulder pads and the colour hot pink, which she named 'shocking pink'. She would later be known for her clothing featuring surrealist designs, even recruiting Salvador Dalí (1904–89) to design fabrics.

The Illustrators

With the growth of the magazine industry and the subsequent increase in press advertising, it was a wonderful era in which to be an illustrator. Fortunately, many skilful illustrators emerged to fill the pages of the new publications. Some of these turned their hand to the crop of fashion magazines that emerged in Paris, bringing a fresh approach to fashion illustration with broad swathes of vivid colour, brilliant line and the posing of the models in real situations, giving life to the designs on show.

Georges Barbier (1882–1932)

Barbier was one of the greatest French illustrators of the twentieth century. He produced book illustrations, costume designs for the cinema and theatre, fans, jewellery, glass, fabrics and wallpaper but, above all, he was revered for his wonderful fashion illustrations which appeared in *Gazette du Bon Ton* (*see page* 108), *Le Jardin des Dames et des Modes*, *Modes et Manières d'Aujourd'hui*, *Femina* and *Vogue*.

Tamara de Lempicka (1898–1980)

Born into a wealthy, aristocratic Polish-Russian family in Moscow in 1898, Tamara de Lempicka became one of the most glamorous artists of her time and one of the best known among those working in the Art Deco style. Hers was an

too had her work, which is now bought for millions of dollars by present-day celebrities such as Jack Nicholson, Madonna and Barbara Streisand (*see left and also page 116*).

Paul Colin (1892–1985)

Paul Colin, one of France's greatest portrait artists, began his career working in the Art Deco style. He is best known for his 1925 poster for the *Revue Nègre*, a stage show starring black American singer, dancer and actress Josephine Baker (1906–75) and featuring a wild new dance: the Charleston. Colin, an aspiring young artist from Nancy in France, launched his spectacular career with this commission and also became Baker's lover.

He capitalized on the new Jazz Age phenomenon by staging the *Bal Nègre* in 1927 – a spectacular event that attracted 3,000 Parisians. Also, in 1929, he published a portfolio of brilliantly coloured lithographs, *Le Tumulte Noire* (the Black Craze), which superbly captured the exuberance of the jazz music and wild dancing that was taking Paris and the rest of the world by storm.

Christian Bérard (1902–49)

Affectionately known as 'Bébé', Bérard first exhibited at the Galerie Druet in 1924 and, by the end of the 1920s, he was influencing several fashion designers such as Christian Dior (1905–57) and Elsa Schiaparelli with whom he worked in the following decade. He would go on to play an important role in the development of theatrical design in the 1930s and 1940s.

Erté (1892–1990)

Russian-born French artist Romain de Tirtoff (Erté) worked in many fields – jewellery, graphic arts, costume and set design and interior decoration. He was contracted to Paul Poiret from 1914 to 1915 and then began work for *Harper's Bazaar*, for which he designed over 200 covers. His work also appeared on the pages of such publications as *The Illustrated London News*, *Ladies' Home Journal* and *Vogue*. He later

elegant, precise style, and by 1925, she had become the most fashionable and expensive portrait painter of her generation, painting Europe's aristocrats and the rich and successful. She led a scandalous life in Paris and had countless affairs with both men and women, resulting in her husband divorcing her in 1931. Meanwhile, she paid little attention to her daughter Kizette, apart from executing a number of memorable portraits of her, such as the beautiful *Kizette en Rose* (*see page* 114) .

In 1939, with war looming and finding herself the wife of a baron, she moved to America where she became the favourite artist of many Hollywood stars, living in style and becoming a famous socialite; in gossip columns of the time, she was dubbed 'the Baroness with the Brush'. Her paintings later went out of fashion for many years, but by the time of her death in 1980, Art Deco had returned to favour and so

Georges Lepape (1887–1971)

In 1911, Paul Poiret commissioned Lepape to illustrate his catalogue, *Les Choses de Paul Poiret* – a seminal piece of Art Deco design that was produced in gold- and silver-highlighted *pochoir* (*see below*). His line drawings with large areas of blues, greens, pinks and yellows appeared in many fashion magazines, including *Gazette du Bon Ton* (*see page 72*) and *Vogue*.

Charles Martin (1884–1934)

As an illustrator, graphic artist, posterist, fashion, costume and ballet and theatre set designer, Charles Martin contributed to most of the major French fashion journals of the time, including *Gazette du Bon Ton*, *Modes et Manières d'Aujourd'hui*, *Journal des Dames et des Modes*, and *Vogue*. He also illustrated books, including a hat collection called *Les Modes en 1912* (*see page 53*).

designed costumes for Radio City Music Hall and the Paris Opera (*see above and also page 49*).

Paul Iribe (1883–1935)

Paul Iribe began as a caricaturist, but in 1908 Paul Poiret commissioned him to create a promotional brochure for his outfits. Using the *pochoir* technique, with its simple lines and flat, abstract swathes of colour, he brilliantly portrayed Poiret's designs. Iribe also worked for Coco Chanel, Jeanne Lanvin, Callot Soeurs and Jacques Doucet (1853–1929), amongst others.

Edouard Halouze (1900–?)

The work of painter, decorator and illustrator Edouard Halouze appeared frequently in *Gazette du Bon Ton* and he took part in an exhibition that was dedicated to 'Fashion as Seen by Painters' at the Musée des Arts Décoratifs in 1920. By 1925, he had developed a unique Cubist style in interiors, costumes and programme covers for the French music halls.

Fashion in the Jazz Age

THE TUBULAR DRESSES THAT HAD BEGUN to be worn during the war remained fashionable after it, giving women the thin, boyish silhouette that was rapidly becoming the desired look. Hemlines that had already climbed above the ankle rose further, and dresses often sported pleats, gathers or slits to facilitate movement. These elements, plus more convenient and manageable short hairstyles, enabled women of the Jazz Age to indulge in the new passion for sporting activity, or to kick up their heels when performing the Charleston or the Black Bottom.

🞜 Waists dropped, further adding to the straight lines that reflected the geometric forms of Art Deco. The optimism of the time was evidenced in the vivid colours that were used in fabrics. Clothes became an expression of women's new experience of the post-war world (*see pages* 68–69).

The Flapper

🞜 Writer F. Scott Fitzgerald – one of the first to use the term – described the typical flapper as 'lovely, expensive and about 19', but this word to describe the new breed of young women was coined by a disapproving, older generation. Nonetheless, the flapper was brash, independent, hedonistic, attractive and often reckless. 'I can't be bothered resisting things I want,' complains Gloria Patch in Fitzgerald's 1922 novel *The Beautiful and Damned*.

🞜 The flapper was a cigarette-smoking, cocktail-guzzling, social butterfly whose provocative behaviour and casual attitude to sex outraged her elders. Moreover, her boyish appearance and distinctive flesh-exposing clothes, with their exotic styles and vibrant colours, caused affront to those who had grown up amidst the more restrained mores of Victorian and Edwardian times (*see page 93*).

The Lifestyle

The flapper lifestyle developed especially in the United States, where a number of actresses (principally Clara Bow, Louise Brooks (1906–85) and Colleen Moore (1899–1988)) became exemplars of the style. Flappers were particularly known for their disdain for all types of authority, although disdain for authority had become a national pastime in the United States following the 1918 introduction of Prohibition. Infraction of the no-alcohol law was universal, and the young learned that the law was there to be broken on occasion.

Other institutionalized beliefs were also being questioned at the time. Religion felt itself to be under threat, especially from Charles Darwin's (1809–82) Theory of Evolution. The arrest of John Thomas Scopes (1900–70), a young biology teacher who broke Tennessee law by lecturing on the Theory of Evolution, was followed by the Scopes Trial, which set modernists against traditionalists, turning the case into a cause célèbre. Fundamentalism was ridiculed during the proceedings, further alienating many people for whom religion was very important, as it represented a bulwark against the forces of change that were prevalent. This led many, including flappers, to question the validity of long-held beliefs and traditions.

The image of the flapper was that of a young woman who, to the horror of her elders, was in the habit of going to jazz clubs. Worse still, she was often unaccompanied (*see page* 110). Once there, she would dance the provocative Black Bottom, the Charleston, the Shimmy or the Bunny Hug. The magazine *The Atlantic Monthly* claimed disparagingly that when flappers danced, they would 'trot like foxes, limp like lame ducks, one-step like cripples, and all to the barbaric yawp of strange instruments which transform the whole scene into a moving-picture of a fancy ball in bedlam'.

When not dancing, the flapper would smoke cigarettes and drink cocktails, if the club happened to be a speakeasy. And even if it was not a drinking den, she would be liable to have brought her own alcohol in a hip flask anyway. She was fast-living and lived her life as though it could be snatched away at any moment – a reflection, perhaps, of the fact that almost an entire generation of young people had indeed had their lives snatched away during the Great War.

At other times, the flapper could be found riding a bicycle, driving a car or playing sports, but always, of course, dressed in the appropriate latest flapper fashions. The car was especially useful because when she was not driving it like a maniac, the flapper could use its back seat for the newly popular sexual activity of petting. Her attitude to sex and relationships was shocking to the older generation. No longer were the rigid mating rituals of Victorian society adhered to. The modern girl attended 'petting parties' where couples 'made out', and sought male company for pleasure and fun, rather than merely for marriage.

Flappers even communicated with each other in their own slang: a man who regularly attended 'petting parties' was a 'snuggle pup'; having to 'see a man about a dog' meant going to buy an alcoholic drink; and approval was expressed by the phrases 'the bee's knees' or 'the cat's pyjamas'. A number of their slang terms are now commonly used in everyday parlance: 'big cheese' means an important person, 'to bump off' means to murder, and 'baloney' means nonsense.

Of course, there were many who railed against the new attitudes. Suffragettes, who had fought for women's right to vote, saw them as vacuous and wondered whether their long struggle had been worth it. On the other hand, others believed

the flapper
to be truly modern.
Liberal writer Dorothy Dunbar
Bromley (1896–1986) described them
as 'New Style' feminists who 'admit that a
full life calls for marriage and children' but also
'are moved by an inescapable inner compulsion to be
individuals in their own right'.

The Look

◦ The typical flapper look is one that conjures up the noise, smells and fun of a 1920s speakeasy. It was known in French as *garçonne* – an appropriate title, given the boyish silhouette to which women began to aspire, as seen in André Edouard Marty's 'Girl on a Swing' (1926, *see page* 111). Many wore a restrictive foundation garment called the 'flattener' over the bust, while others wound strips of cloth around it in order to render it virtually nonexistent, thus achieving a youthful, boyish physique. This, coupled with straight waists dropped to the hipline, allowed the 'tube dress' to become the height of fashion; such attire ignored the natural curves of the female form.

◦ Although the full expression of the flapper look – straight waists, hair cut in a bob and hemlines hovering daringly around the knee – was not established until around 1926, elements of it had already begun to be seen before the war. In 1913, American opera singer Lillian Nordica (1857–1914) described 'a thin little flapper of a girl donning a skirt in which she can hardly take a step, extinguishing all but her little white teeth with a dumpy bucket of a hat, and tripping down Fifth Avenue'.

◦ At the start of the 1920s, the hemline rose no more than a few inches. From 1925 to 1927, however, it rose to just below the knee, overlapping – only just – the top of the flapper's rolled stockings. In certain situations, the knee became visible, which was regarded as risqué – not that the flapper really cared. The legs were clothed in stockings made of rayon – a semi-synthetic fibre that acted as a cheap alternative to the more expensive silk – and were often worn rolled over a garter belt.

◦ The flapper's predecessor, the Gibson Girl, wore her long, lush hair piled on top of her head. It was startling, therefore, when the next generation cut their hair very short, wearing it initially in a bob and later perhaps in a 'shingle' or 'Eton' cut. The shingle cut was slicked down with the front and sides cut to cover the ears. At the back, the hair was cut at an angle, into layers of short fringe at the neck that resembled the shingles of a roof, giving the cut its name. At the sides, it was also cut on a slant with a curl covering the earlobe. It was parted in the centre and could sometimes be waved. The Eton crop was slightly more radical: cut close to the top of the head and flattened, often using Brilliantine – the men's hair cream. It was

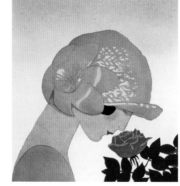

the style worn by the immensely popular American dancer and singer Josephine Baker. The drama of this new hairstyle is evident in Georges Lepape's 'The Visit', taken from a 1925 issue of *Gazette du Bon Ton* showing dress and coat designs by Jeanne Lanvin (*see page* 100).

◦ Dramatically short hairstyles suited the wearing of the close-fitting, bell-shaped, felt cloche hat, as seen in *Gazette du Bon Ton* in June 1924 (*see left and also page* 85).

Flappers wore make-up – rouge, face powder, eyeliner and vibrant lipstick – which had previously been associated only with women considered to be of loose morals. The magazine *The New Republic* described the typical flapper as 'frankly, heavily made up, not to imitate nature, but for an altogether artificial effect – pallor mortis, poisonously scarlet lips, richly ringed eyes – the latter looking not so much debauched (which is the intention) as diabetic' (*see page* 66).

The Clothes

It has been estimated that between 1913 and 1928 the amount of fabric used to dress a woman fell from 17.5 m (19¼ yards) to just 6.4 m (7 yards) and consisted more often than not of a thin frock worn over a brassiere, a pair of knickers and silk or rayon stockings. Flappers were recognizable from their style of dress, which emerged out of French fashion (*see page* 56) and, in particular, what was designed by Coco Chanel, who championed the 'garçonne' look.

In order to achieve the flapper look, restrictive corsets that made the waist thinner in order to emphasize the hips and bust became a thing of the past, even though women could be arrested before the war for not wearing them. Flappers often wore simple bust bodices or a bra, such as the popular Symington Side Lacer, to flatten the chest and also hold it still while they were dancing the Charleston. Large breasts were actually perceived as displaying a lack of sophistication. Softer, suppler corsets that reached to the hips were worn and served to smooth the entire torso, giving wearers a straight up-and-down look – all curves banished. Silk camiknickers, or 'step-ins', and transparent stockings, rolled beneath the knee, replaced thick, black stockings and bloomers. In terms of materials, thick wool, starched cotton and whalebone were replaced by light silk and newly developed synthetic fabrics such as rayon.

The uniform of the flapper consisted of the straight-line chemise topped with the ever-present cloche hat, pulled low on the forehead and covering the face to the extent that

young women had to hold their heads at an angle to see where they were going. Dresses were low-waisted and full at the hemline. Coats were long until 1926 and were usually wrap-over in style, with just one side fastening. Linings of coats were often co-ordinated with dress fabrics and women also wore fur shawl collars (*see page* 84).

Meanwhile, with hemlines rising, shoes assumed a new importance. They were now mass-produced and were more readily affordable than before. The 'Mary Jane' ankle strap button shoe was the predominant style of the decade. And no flapper outfit was complete without bangles and long strings of pearls, ready to be swung around and rattled when dancing the Charleston or the Black Bottom (*see pages* 88–89).

The Sporty Girl

In the early 1900s, it was still considered unbecoming for a woman to take part in competitive sports. The modern woman of the 1920s, however, was keen to take part in the sporting revolution that was sweeping the world and 'sporty girls' could be seen playing tennis or golf, or having fun on the ski slopes.

Naturally, these new pastimes required the right outfits, which had to be comfortable and functional without sacrificing style and elegance.

The Lifestyle

☙ The booming economy led to greater financial stability and this, coupled with the growth in air travel, led those who could afford it to take an interest in exotic journeys. Within months of the end of the Great War, in fact, the Swiss ski resort of St Moritz had once again become popular for skating and skiing, and during the cold, winter months, the social elite could be found in the warmer climes of the French Riviera, Egypt and North Africa (*see pages* 107 and 119). Women moved into non-traditional roles; some even took advantage of the new fascination with sport, until that time traditionally dominated by males, by playing tennis, skiing, bicycling, sailing, golfing and swimming (*see pages* 78 and 117).

☙ Earlier in the twentieth century it had not been considered important for women to win at competitive sports, as it was believed that it made them seem less feminine. They could take part, but the lack of competitiveness was reflected in the way the clothes they wore during such activities were designed: for anything but practicality. In the 1920s, however, practical clothing that still retained style began to be designed.

☙ The appearance of women in track and field sports at the Olympic Games during the 1920s encouraged female participation in competitive sports, as did the great success of the French tennis player Suzanne Lenglen, who won six Wimbledon Ladies' titles between 1919 and 1926 and was dressed exquisitely by Jean Patou.

The Look

☙ Sporting activities often took place in private clubs that, of course, demanded the appropriate attire for whichever sport the 'sporty girl' was playing. The look to which she aspired was one of comfort and a kind of fluid elegance, as achieved by clothing that was not constricting and allowed movement, whether it be the swing of a golf club or a tennis racquet. Comfort and the ability to move freely were all (*see left*).

☙ The craze for outdoor sporting activities was encouraged by scientific reports that championed the health-giving properties of sunlight. Until that time, it had been felt that the only reason for having a tan was outdoor work, which implied that a person was of a lower class. It was Coco Chanel who helped women to dispense with this prejudice, launching the new tanned look after being accidentally sunburned while on holiday on the French Riviera. Meanwhile, Parisians loved singer Josephine Baker's dark skin and tried to emulate it.

The Clothes

- 'Sporty girl' clothing had to be both functional and beautiful, although the same thing could be said about a great deal of Art Deco clothing (*see page* 139). Coco Chanel was the queen of this type of simple, streamlined, elegant and comfortable clothing, and the look that she created for women seemed effortless. Similarly, Jean Patou, with his shop Sports Corner that specifically sold sportswear to women, was at the forefront of satisfying the new demand for ladies' leisurewear.

- Patou combined jersey with the strict lines that could be found in the designs of wartime clothes, and established himself as Chanel's main rival in this type of clothing. He designed beautiful outfits for the beach and for hill climbing, but he is probably best known for the designs he created for the French tennis star Suzanne Lenglen – especially the all-white outfit with a bright orange bandeau that he created for her to wear at Wimbledon in 1922 and which provides one of the abiding images of the entire decade. Lenglen also wore Patou designs off-court, making her the first sports star to promote a fashion house.

- Sonia Delaunay (1885–1979) designed brightly embroidered beachwear, sporting abstract designs and striking colour schemes that would influence mainstream fashion (*see right*).

- Pyjamas, originating with the Ballet Russes and the harem pantaloons designed by Paul Poiret, became items to be worn on the beach or for lounging about at home. They often bore exotic, hand-painted motifs and were especially prized by the avant-garde.

- Pleated skirts or wide-legged trousers were required for some sports such as golf, while masculine, angular jackets often complemented them. The safari-style jacket and wide-brimmed sunhats became fashionable for the outdoors (*see page* 77).

- Some of the lightweight fabrics used in sportswear in order to allow maximum freedom, such as jersey, cotton, morocco and

silk, also began to appear in everyday fashion collections. The colour combinations found on tennis and sailing outfits – white and navy, white and red, and yellow and green – also began to be used in everyday outfits.

The Silver Screen Goddess

- It was only around 1910 that the stars of films first had their names shown in the credits. By 1920, however, it was these names that often sold a movie to its prospective audience. Charlie Chaplin was the biggest star in the Hollywood firmament, but there were many great names that attracted millions of people to movie theatres every week, such as Douglas Fairbanks, John Gilbert and Buster Keaton.

- One of the movie men's greatest marketing tools, however, were the legendary screen goddesses: actresses who were objects of worship to an adoring audience and whose every move was followed in the magazines of the day. The pages of Hollywood movie magazines such as *Photoplay* or *Motion Picture* thrilled to the latest movie news and interviews with screen sirens such as Lillian Gish (1893–1993), Louise Brooks, Clara Bow, Norma Talmadge (1894–1957), Greta Garbo (1905–90) and Theda Bara (1885–1955). Their lavish lifestyles were envied, and their make-up and clothes were analysed by women everywhere who tried to bring a little bit of Hollywood glamour to their own wardrobes (*see page* 129).

The Lifestyle

⤳ Mystery was an important element in the life of the female silent movie star. Theda Bara, for instance, was born Theodosia Goodman and the studio that employed her described her as the daughter of an eastern potentate, whereas she was actually the daughter of a tailor from Cincinnati, Ohio. The studio aimed to portray her, both on and off the screen, as a 'vamp' – a type of sexual vampire or *femme fatale*. She was photographed with skulls and snakes, and wearing beaded and fringed outfits that sought to shock and outrage.

⤳ Stars such as Louise Brooks, whose freckled face and dramatic physical features were loved by the silent movie camera, starred alongside such names as W.C. Fields (1880–1946), Jean Arthur (1900–91) and William Powell (1892–1954) in 24 films between 1925 and 1938. She mixed with the rich and famous of her time: glamorous socialites, wealthy industrialists, newspaper magnates and famous and successful writers and artists such as F. Scott Fitzgerald, chronicler of the Jazz Age. Brooks was stunningly beautiful and the very embodiment of the flapper, with her devil-may-care attitude to relationships and sex. Her stunning looks gained her work as a model as well as an actress and her face regularly graced advertisements.

⤳ The stars lived in fabulous mansions in Beverley Hills: a community that had been established in 1906. In 1919, swashbuckling movie star Douglas Fairbanks and his wife Mary Pickford announced that they would be building their dream home – to be called 'Pickfair' – there. Will Rogers (1879–1935), Harold Lloyd, John Barrymore (1882–1942), Robert Montgomery (1904–81) and Miriam Hopkins (1902–72) followed suit. It was the start of a land boom and the arrival of Beverley Hills as the home of the stars. Sumptuous mansions with grand entrances, manicured grounds and large swimming pools hid behind massive gates and high walls. Lavish parties would be thrown at these properties, attended by the great and the good, where the dances of the time would be performed with wild abandon and jazz would echo through the spacious rooms.

⤳ Stars would dine out at places such as the Café Montmartre, a swanky café and nightclub owned by European restaurateur Eddie Brandstatter, on Hollywood Boulevard and Highland Avenue, which was described by one newspaper as 'the center of Hollywood life, where everybody worthwhile goes to see and be seen'. The nights to be there were Wednesdays and Fridays – if you could bear to wait in the long queues to gain entry – when diners could watch the doyenne of gossip columnists Louella Parsons move from table to table in search of juicy bits of movieland tittle-tattle to spice up her column the following day.

⤳ Even though Prohibition was in force, everyone brought a full hip flask and, if the booze ran out, there was a bootlegger on the premises ready to top you up, but this came at a price. Meanwhile, there was dancing – there was always dancing in the 1920s – and in between dances, diners could watch a floor show in which, needless to say, other people danced.

There was even dancing at lunchtime when the Montmartre featured a 'bachelors' table' of good-looking young men who were available to dance with the ladies who lunched (*see above*).

When Brandstatter opened a private club – the Embassy – for Hollywood stars, however, the stars naturally chose to go there rather than be gawped at at the Montmartre. Sadly, with the stars opting to dine in private, ordinary people had no real reason to go to the Montmartre and the business went downhill.

Away from the glamour and glitz, Hollywood in the 1920s also had a seamier side. In the face of a number of scandals featuring some well-known stars, it earned the epithet 'the Sodom of the western world', especially after the death of former Ziegfeld girl Olive Thomas (1894–1920) – known as 'the most beautiful girl in the world'. Thomas starred in the popular movie *The Flapper* (1920), which was possibly the first time the term was used in the context of a modern girl who dressed in a particular way. She died after swallowing bichloride of mercury – the medicine that her abusive husband had been prescribed for the syphilis from which he had been suffering. It remains unclear as to why she swallowed the drug. Hers was Hollywood's first celebrity funeral, and it was watched by thousands of movie fans.

Superstar Mabel Normand (1892–1930), meanwhile, was one of many who suffered from a serious cocaine habit. She would become a suspect in the mysterious murder of William Desmond Taylor (1872–1922), who was one of the biggest directors in Hollywood at the time.

Mostly, though, the screen goddess's life was a succession of extravagant premieres and even more extravagant parties. And, now and then, a movie would be made.

The Look

✿ They were sultry and unobtainable, described as goddesses and often behaved like them too. The divas of 1920s silent films, oozing sensuality and sexual promise, were like creatures from another planet to moviegoers, who had just emerged firstly from the Victorian era and then the desperate war years. They were serpentine beauties who shimmered on the silver screen and seemed to float above the red carpet at the film premieres they graced with their ethereal presence (*see above*). They wore fabulous clothes, often designed by the great French couturiers whose designs they would buy in bulk.

✿ One of the truly great silent actresses was Mary Pickford: the wife of Douglas Fairbanks and a very powerful Hollywood figure. However, the fascination for her look – that of a childlike waif with her hair in ringlets – waned as the Twenties

wore on, and she was replaced by younger actresses who had embraced the flapper lifestyle and look.

✿ Clara Bow came to personify the 1920s, earning the nickname 'The "It" Girl' from her role in the film *It*. In 1924, however, she disassociated herself from flapper roles, telling the *Los Angeles Times*, 'No more flappers … they have served their purpose … people are tired of soda-pop love affairs'.

✿ That left the most iconic of all the young actresses of the decade: Louise Brooks. The Dutch bob looked like a jet-black helmet on her, but along with the actress Colleen Moore, they made it the hairstyle of the Twenties. Millions of women copied it in an effort to steal just a little of her astonishing, dark, exotic beauty. In *Pandora's Box*, the famous 1929 film directed by G.W. Pabst, she wore a stunning bronze lamé dress trimmed with fur designed by Jean Patou (*see pages* 115 and 125).

It was not just the hairstyle and the clothing that helped make Louise Brooks the archetypal flapper. She also possessed the rebellious attitude and the independence of spirit that characterized the young women of her time and made her so disliked by the Hollywood elite.

The Clothes

Of course, working in the monochrome world of film brought problems, and designers were forced to resort to shiny or textured fabrics to achieve the required visual effect. That resulted in the use of lamés, sequins and boas that would stand out and give some depth to the clothes being worn. The only colours that would be seen by the viewer, of course, were black and white, which led to the exploitation of the black and white spectrum, ranging from brilliant-white platinum to shiny black. However, the sharpness and precision required in both couture and hairstyle by black-and-white films found their way into mainstream fashion (*see page* 76).

Budgets were always tight and producers were reluctant to lavish precious dollars on *haute couture* dresses for their leading actresses. In order to maintain their image of being at the forefront of the latest fashions, the more successful actresses were forced, therefore, to purchase dresses directly from the designers, using their own money. Some travelled to Paris specifically for this purpose and Mary Pickford, one of the leading silent film stars of the time, was a regular visitor to the salons of the major designers. During one of those trips, she reportedly bought 50 dresses, many of which were worn in her films.

Glamour, sultriness and mystery prevailed in silent films and their female stars used their shape and clothing in a highly expressive way, wearing clingy items made of light fabrics such as satin, chiffon and taffeta, with long hemlines that displayed their mermaid outlines to best advantage (*see far left and also page* 86). Off-screen, they were little different. Wealth and luxury were suggested by sumptuous and hugely expensive fur coats and wraps, or stoles, made of fox fur and often with the

animal's head still attached – a bizarre prospect for the modern woman, but the height of fashion in the 1920s.

American actresses were the first to create their own individual styles. Lillian Gish was known for her pastel muslin dresses and Greta Garbo, in her cape and low-pulled cloche, became the embodiment of 'wanting to be alone', as well as the epitome of fashion in late 1920s American cinema.

Eventually, however, it all came to an end. In 1930, Coco Chanel was paid a million dollars to design clothes for Gloria Swanson (1899–1983) to wear in the film *Tonight or Never*. When the film was screened, though, it was generally agreed that the designs of this greatest of couturiers were 'not glamorous enough' for Hollywood.

Fashion, it seemed, had moved on.

The Masterpieces

Georges Lepape (1887–1971)
The Turban, illustration from *Les Choses de Paul Poiret*, 1911
© ADAGP, Paris and DACS, London 2012/The Bridgeman Art Library
Medium: Hand-coloured lithograph

Georges Lepape (1887–1971)
'Sorbet' dress, fashion plate for an evening gown by Paul Poiret,
Gazette du Bon Ton, 1912
© ADAGP, Paris and DACS, London 2012/The Bridgeman Art Library
Medium: Unknown

Erté (Romain de Tirtoff) (1892–1990)
Loge de Theatre, based on an original design, 1912
© Sevenarts Limited
Medium: Embossed serigraph

Georges Lepape (1887–1971)
Au Clair de la Lune, fashion plate for an evening gown by Paul Poiret,
Gazette du Bon Ton, 1913
© ADAGP, Paris and DACS, London 2012/The Bridgeman Art Library
Medium: Watercolour

(Previous page) **Georges Barbier (1882–1932)**
Isola Bella, **designs for evening dresses by Redfern,**
Gazette du Bon Ton, **1914**
© Private Collection/The Bridgeman Art Library
Medium: *Pochoir*

Artist unknown
Fashion plate for Paul Poiret gowns,
Gazette du Bon Ton, **1914**
© Victoria & Albert Museum, London, UK/The Bridgeman Art Library
Medium: Colour lithograph

Erté (Romain de Tirtoff) (1892–1990)
New York Robe, **costume design**
for theatre producer George White, 1917
© Sevenarts Limited
Medium: Gouache on paper

Erté (Romain de Tirtoff) (1892–1990)
Cape à la Russe, derived from original design for *New York Robe*, 1917
© Sevenarts Limited
Medium: Embossed serigraph

Georges Barbier (1882–1932)
Les Trois Graces, illustration from the almanac *La Guirlande des Mois*, 1918
© Bibliothèque des Arts Décoratifs, Paris, France/The Bridgeman Art Library
Medium: Colour lithograph

LES TROIS GRACES.

Erté (Romain de Tirtoff) (1892–1990)
Winter in Paris, **based on a drawing for** *Harper's Bazaar,* **1919**
© Sevenarts Limited
Medium: Embossed serigraph

Erté (Romain de Tirtoff) (1892–1990)
Costume for the actress and singer Gaby Deslys, based on an original design, 1919
© Sevenarts Limited
Medium: Lithograph

Erté (Romain de Tirtoff) (1892–1990)
New Bridges for the Seven Seas, **design for the cover of** *Harper's Bazaar,* 1919
© Sevenarts Limited
Medium: Gouache

Erté (Romain de Tirtoff) (1892–1990)
The Salon, **design for** *Harper's Bazaar,* 1919
© Sevenarts Limited
Medium: Gouache

Georges Barbier (1882–1932)
Midnight! (or *The Fashionable Apartment*),
illustration from the almanac *Le Bonheur du Jour, ou Les Grâces à la Mode,* **1920**
© Private Collection/The Bridgeman Art Library
Medium: *Pochoir*

Charles Martin (1848–1934)
Picnic and Fishing Scene, illustration from *Sports et divertissements, c.* 1920
© ADAGP, Paris and DACS, London 2012/The Bridgeman Art Library
Medium: *Pochoir*

Georges Barbier (1882–1932), engraved by Henri Reidel
The Backless Dress, illustration from the almanac
Le Bonheur du Jour, ou Les Grâces à la Mode, 1920
© Private Collection/The Bridgeman Art Library
Medium: Colour lithograph

Erté (Romain de Tirtoff) (1892–1990)
Fantasia, based on a design for the cover of *Harper's Bazaar*, 1920
© Sevenarts Limited
Medium: Serigraph

Georges Barbier (1882–1932), engraved by Henri Reidel
Love is Blind, illustration from the almanac
Le Bonheur du Jour, ou Les Grâces à la Mode, 1920
© Private Collection/The Bridgeman Art Library
Medium: Colour lithograph

Charles Martin (1848–1934)
Sledging, illustration from *Sports et divertissements, c.* 1920
© ADAGP, Paris and DACS, London 2012/The Bridgeman Art Library
Medium: *Pochoir*

Georges Barbier (1882–1932), engraved by Henri Reidel
At The Lido, illustration from the almanac
Le Bonheur du Jour, ou Les Grâces à la Mode, 1920
© Private Collection/The Bridgeman Art Library
Medium: Colour lithograph

Georges Lepape (1887–1971)
Day Dress, 1920
© ADAGP, Paris and DACS, London 2012/The Bridgeman Art Library
Medium: Colour lithograph

Charles Martin (1848–1934)
Evening Wedding on the Balcony, c. 1920
© ADAGP, Paris and DACS, London 2012/The Bridgeman Art Library
Medium: Stencil on paper

André Edouard Marty (1882–1974)
Brise du Large, **fashion plate for a honeymoon dress,** *Gazette du Bon Ton*, **1921**
© ADAGP, Paris and DACS, London 2012/The Bridgeman Art Library
Medium: Colour lithograph

BRISE DU LARGE

ROBE DE VOYAGE DE NOCES, DE DŒUILLET

AU LOUP !

ROBE EN "FLEURS DES BLÉS" ET ROBE EN "GUIRLANDE FLEURIE", DE RODIER

Nº 4 de la Gazette du Bon Ton.   Année 1921. — Planche.

Georges Barbier (1882–1932)
The Judgement of Paris, **fashion plate for** *haute couture* **dresses, 1923**
© Private Collection/The Bridgeman Art Library
Medium: *Pochoir*

André Edouard Marty (1882–1974)
Au Loup!, **fashion plate for dresses by Rodier,** *Gazette du Bon Ton,* **1921**
© ADAGP, Paris and DACS, London 2012/The Bridgeman Art Library
Medium: Colour lithograph

Oui!

A L'OASIS

ou

LA VOUTE PNEUMATIQUE

ROBE DU SOIR. DE PAUL POIRET

7 de la Gazette du Bon Ton.   Année 1921. — Planche 53

Georges Barbier (1882–1932)
Oui!, illustration from the almanac *Falbalas & Fanfreluches*, **1921**
© Private Collection/The Bridgeman Art Library
Medium: Colour lithograph

André Edouard Marty (1882–1974)
À L'Oasis ou La Voute Pneumatique, fashion plate for an evening gown
by Paul Poiret, *Gazette du Bon Ton*, **1921**
© ADAGP, Paris and DACS, London 2012/The Bridgeman Art Library
Medium: Colour lithograph

"QUE PENSEZ-VOUS DES SIX?"

OU

ON NE PEUT PAS ÊTRE TRANQUILLE

ROBE DU SOIR, DE PAUL POIRET

Erté (1892–1990)
Gala, based in a original design
for Mrs William Randolph Hearst, 1921
© Sevenarts Limited
Medium: Embossed serigraph

André Edouard Marty (1882–1974)
***Que Pensez-Vous des Six?*, fashion plate for an evening gown**
by Paul Poiret, *Gazette du Bon Ton*, 1921
© ADAGP, Paris and DACS, London 2012/The Bridgeman Art Library
Medium: Colour lithograph

(Next page) **Artist unknown**
***The Seaside*, fashion plate**
from *Art, Goût, Beauté*, 1920s
© John Jesse, London, UK/The Bridgeman Art Library
Medium: *Pochoir*

Georges Lepape (1887–1971)
Illustration from *Les Choses de Paul Poiret*, 1911
© ADAGP, Paris and DACS, London 2012/The Bridgeman Art Library
Medium: Colour lithograph

Pierre Brissaud (1885–1964)
Tu Vas Trop Vite, Maman!, **fashion plate for designs by Jeanne Lanvin, 1921**
© Bibliothèque des Arts Décoratifs, Paris, France/The Bridgeman Art Library
Medium: Colour Lithograph

Georges Lepape (1887–1971)
Fashion plate for a winter great-coat by Gilles, *Gazette du Bon Ton,* **1922**
© ADAGP, Paris and DACS, London 2012/The Bridgeman Art Library
Medium: *Pochoir*

André Edouard Marty (1882–1974)
La Belle Affligee, **fashion plate for an evening dress by Paul Poiret,** *Gazette du Bon Ton,* **1922**
© ADAGP, Paris and DACS, London 2012/The Bridgeman Art Library
Medium: Colour lithograph

Artist unknown
Arriving at the Party, fashion plate depicting evening gowns, *Art, Goût, Beauté,* 1920s
© Private Collection/The Bridgeman Art Library
Medium: *Pochoir*

Georges Barbier (1882–1932)
Incantation, illustration from the almanac *Falbalas & Fanfreluches,* 1922
© Private Collection/The Bridgeman Art Library
Medium: *Pochoir*

Erté (Romain de Tirtoff) (1892–1990)
Opening Night, based on a design for *Harper's Bazaar*, 1921
© Sevenarts Limited
Medium: Embossed serigraph

Georges Barbier (1882–1932)
Amalfi, fashion plate for a dress by Charles Worth,
Gazette du Bon Ton, 1922
© Private Collection/The Bridgeman Art Library
Medium: *Pochoir*

Art - Goût - Beauté

Artist unknown
Skating Elegance, fashion plate from *Art, Goût, Beauté*, 1920s
© Private Collection/The Bridgeman Art Library
Medium: *Pochoir*

Georges Barbier (1882–1932)
The Style of Shawls, illustration from the almanac *Falbalas & Fanfreluches*, 1922
© Private Collection/The Bridgeman Art Library
Medium: Colour lithograph

L'OFFRANDE DU POÈTE

OU

" JE NE SAIS COMMENT VOUS REMERCIER "

ROBE D'APRÈS-MIDI, DE BEER

VESTON BORDÉ, POUR L'APRÈS-MIDI, DE KRIEGCK

Eduardo Garcia Benito (1891–1953)
L'Offrande du Poète, fashion plate for an afternoon dress by Gustav Beer,
and a trimmed men's afternoon jacket by Kriegck, *Gazette du Bon Ton,* 1922
© Bibliothèque des Arts Décoratifs, Paris, France/The Bridgeman Art Library
Medium: Colour lithograph

Georges Barbier (1882–1932)
The Tango, c. 1920s
© Private Collection/The Bridgeman Art Library
Medium: Pen, ink and watercolour on paper

LA GLACE

OU

UN COUP D'OEIL EN PASSANT

MANTEAU DU SOIR, DE PAUL POIRET

N° 6 de la Gazette du Bon Ton.

Année 1922. — Planche 47

'Thayaht' Ernesto Michahelles (1893–1959)
Souvenir de Paques a Rome, **fashion plate depicting an afternoon dress**
by Madeleine Vionnet, *Gazette du Bon Ton,* **1922**
© Private Collection/The Bridgeman Art Library
Medium: Colour lithograph

André Edouard Marty (1882–1974)
La Glace, **fashion plate for an evening coat by Paul Poiret,**
Gazette du Bon Ton, **1922**
© ADAGP, Paris and DACS, London 2012/The Bridgeman Art Library
Medium: Colour lithograph

Georges Barbier (1882–1932)
Leaving for the Casino, **fashion plate for an evening coat by Charles Worth,**
Gazette du Bon Ton, **1923**
© Private Collection/The Bridgeman Art Library
Medium: Colour lithograph

P. Dumas-Boudreau (*fl.* 1923)
At the Art Gallery, **fashion plate for dresses by Christoff von Drecoll and Bernard,**
Art, Goût, Beauté, **1923**
© Bibliothèque des Arts Décoratifs, Paris, France/The Bridgeman Art Library
Medium: *Pochoir*

ELLE VIENT. — *Robe d'après-midi en velours marron "Cambridge" garni de fourrure.*

Création Drecoll

TENTATION. — *Robe d'après-midi enroulée en crêpe "Phili A. G. B." chamois.*

Création Bernard

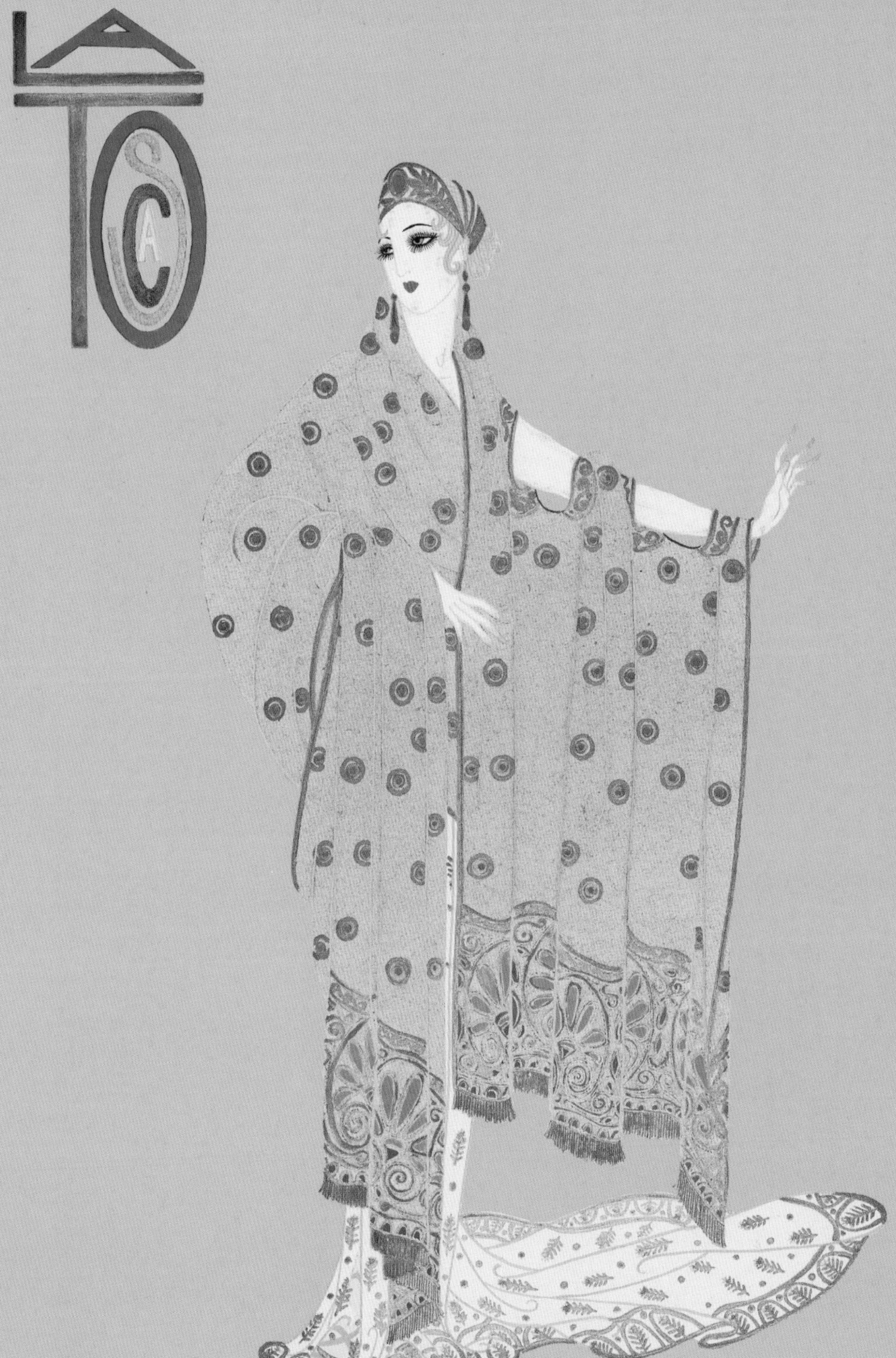
LA TOSCA

Erté (Romain de Tirtoff) (1892–1990)
La Tosca, design for Ganna Walska,
Chicago Opera Company, 1920
© Sevenarts Limited
Medium: Colour lithograph

André Edouard Marty (1882–1974)
The Scent of Roses, fashion plate for a hat
by Marthe Callot, *Gazette du Bon Ton*, 1924
© ADAGP, Paris and DACS, London 2012/The Bridgeman Art Library
Medium: Colour lithograph

(Next page) **Georges Barbier (1882–1932)**
Éventails, illustration from the almanac *Le Bonheur du
Jour, ou Les Grâces à la Mode*, 1924
© Collection Kharbine-Tapabor, Paris, France/
The Bridgeman Art Library
Medium: Colour lithograph

Georges Barbier (1882–1932)
Le Feu, **illustration from the almanac** *Falbalas & Fanfreluches*, 1925
© Private Collection/The Bridgeman Art Library
Medium: *Pochoir*

Artist unknown
Evening at the Casino, **fashion plate for dresses made from**
'Crepes Beauté, Premier Rayon', *Art, Goût, Beauté*, **1920s**
© Private Collection/The Bridgeman Art Library
Medium: *Pochoir*

AUX ACCACIAS...

INTRÉPIDE. — *Robe de tricot de laine multicolore.*

Création Bernard

TIRELIRE. — *Robe de drap noir incrusté de drap beige brodé de couleurs vives.*

Création Paul Poiret

AFFRANCHI. — *Moire marron garnie de crêpe blanc.*

Création Martial et Armand

BAVIÈRE. — *Robe en velours noir bordé de bouillonnés de velours vert.*

Création Paul Poiret

Georges Barbier (1882–1932)
The Swing, illustration from the almanac *Falbalas & Fanfreluches*, 1924
© Private Collection/The Bridgeman Art Library
Medium: *Pochoir*

Roger Chastel (1887–1981)
Fashion Show, **fashion plate from** *Gazette du Bon Ton,* **1924**
© Bibliothèque des Arts Décoratifs, Paris, France/The Bridgeman Art Library
Medium: Colour lithograph

La Robe Couleur de Lune

Georges Barbier (1882–1932)
The Theorbo Player, **fashion plate for an evening coat by Jeanne Paquin,**
Gazette du Bon Ton, **1914**
© Private Collection/The Bridgeman Art Library
Medium: Colour lithograph

Erté (Romain de Tirtoff) (1892–1990)
Monaco, **based on a design in** *Harper's Bazaar* **for an evening coat, 1920**
Medium: Embossed serigraph

LA VISITE

ROBES ET MANTEAUX, DE JEANNE LANVIN

Modèles déposés. Reproduction interdite.

la Gazette.

Année 1924-1925.

Georges Lepape (1887–1971)
La Visite, fashion plate for dress and coat designs by Jeanne Lanvin,
Gazette du Bon Ton, 1925
© ADAGP, Paris and DACS, London 2012/The Bridgeman Art Library
Medium: Colour lithograph

Georges Barbier (1882–1932)
Summer, illustration from the almanac *Falbalas & Fanfreluches*, 1925
© Private Collection/The Bridgeman Art Library
Medium: *Pochoir*

Feodor Stepanovich Rojankovsky (Rojan) (1891–1970)
Lady at the Races, 1920s
© Private Collection//The Bridgeman Art Library
Medium: Colour lithograph

Georges Barbier (1882–1932)
Winter, illustration from the almanac *Falbalas & Fanfreluches*, 1925
© Private Collection/The Bridgeman Art Library
Medium: Colour lithograph

Sylvia Bergin
Stylish Lady, **1920s**
© Private Collection/The Bridgeman Art Library
Medium: Watercolour on paper

Le Style Moderne

Don Mlle Bucquet. Oct. 1937. Env. 741

Umberto Brunelleschi (1879–1949)
Le Style Moderne, c. 1925
© Bibliothèque des Arts Décoratifs, Paris, France/The Bridgeman Art Library
Medium: Colour lithograph

Georges Barbier (1882–1932)
Les Modes, **fashion plate for dresses by Paul Poiret,** *c.* **1920s**
© Private Collection/The Bridgeman Art Library
Medium: Colour lithograph

Artist unknown
The Romance of Rail Travel, **fashion plate from** *Art, Goût, Beauté,* **1920s**
© Private Collection/The Bridgeman Art Library
Medium: *Pochoir*

Georges Barbier (1882–1932)
La Belle Personne, fashion plate for a Charles Worth evening dress,
Gazette du Bon Ton, 1925
© Bibliothèque des Arts Décoratifs, Paris, France/The Bridgeman Art Library
Medium: Colour lithograph

Georges Lepape (1887–1971)
Bride, cover of *Femina*, 1926
© ADAGP, Paris and DACS, London 2012/The Bridgeman Art Library
Medium: Engraving

Artist unknown
At the Dance, fashion plate from *Art, Goût, Beauté,* 1920s
© Private Collection/The Bridgeman Art Library
Medium: *Pochoir*

André Edouard Marty (1882–1974)
Girl on a Swing, 1926
© Private Collection/© DACS 2012/The Bridgeman Art Library
Medium: Watercolour on paper

(Next page) **Artist unknown**
Passengers on a Liner, fashion plate for dresses by Jean
Patou and Lucien Lelong, *Art, Goût, Beauté* 1926
© Bibliothèque des Arts Décoratifs, Paris, France/The Bridgeman Art Library
Medium: *Pochoir*

Tamara de Lempicka (1898–1980)
Kizette en Rose, **1926**
© ADAGP, Paris and DACS, London 2012/The Bridgeman Art Library
Medium: Oil on canvas

Léon Bénigni (1892–1948)
Outdoor Evening Dress, fashion plate for evening wear by Jean Patou,
Art, Goût, Beauté, 1926
© Bibliothèque des Arts Décoratifs, Paris, France/The Bridgeman Art Library
Medium: Colour lithograph

Tamara de Lempicka (1898–1980)
Young Girl in Green, **1927**
© ADAGP, Paris and DACS, London 2012/The Bridgeman Art Library
Medium: Oil on canvas

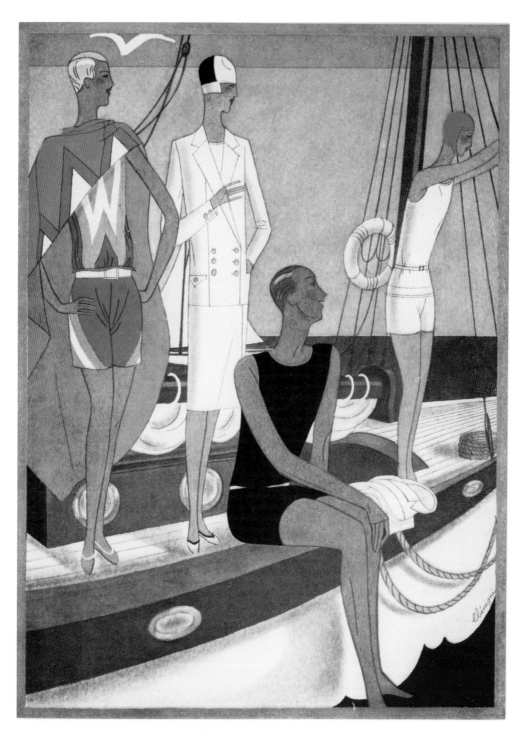

Léon Bénigni (1892–1948)
Summer Life on the Yacht, **fashion plate for bathing and yachting wear**
designed by Jane Régny, *Femina,* **1927**
© Private Collection/The Bridgeman Art Library
Medium: Colour lithograph

Erté (Romain de Tirtoff) (1892–1990)
Manhattan Mary, **costume design for the play** *Manhattan Mary*,
produced by George White, 1927
© Sevenarts Limited
Medium: Gouache

Léon Bénigni (1892–1948)
Le Goût Moderne sur La Croisette, fashionable people strolling on the
Croisette Promenade in Cannes, fashion plate from *Femina*, 1927
© Private Collection/The Bridgeman Art Library
Medium: Colour lithograph

Erté (Romain de Tirtoff) (1892–1990)
Nightclub Scene, costume design for the play *Manhattan Mary*,
produced by George White, 1927
© Sevenarts Limited
Medium: Gouache

Erté (Romain de Tirtoff) (1892–1990)
Queen of the Night, 1975
© Sevenarts Limited
Medium: Gouache

Léon Bénigni (1892–1948)
The Miramar at Cannes, **fashion plate from** *Femina,* **1928**
© Private Collection/The Bridgeman Art Library
Medium: Colour lithograph

Erté (Romain de Tirtoff) (1892–1990)
Aphrodite, **based on a costume design for** *Les Idoles* **at the Folies Bergère, 1924**
© Sevenarts Limited
Medium: Embossed serigraph

Léon Bénigni (1892–1948)
Recevoir sur Son Yacht est à Cannes Un Plaisir Raffiné, **fashion plate for an evening dress by House of Callot Soeurs, 1928**
© Private Collection/The Bridgeman Art Library
Medium: Colour lithograph

LE POUF

ROBE DU SOIR, DE PAUL POIRET

N° 7 de la Gazette. Année 1924 Planche 38

Modèle déposé. Reproduction interdite.

André Edouard Marty (1882–1974)
Le Pouf, **fashion plate for an evening dress by Paul Poiret,** *Gazette du Bon Ton*, **1924**
© ADAGP, Paris and DACS, London 2012/The Bridgeman Art Library
Medium: Colour lithograph

Erté (Romain de Tirtoff) (1892–1990)
Feather Gown, based on a design for *Le Réveil des Elégances Parisiennes*, 1919
© Sevenarts Limited
Medium: Embossed serigraph

Tamara de Lempicka (1898–1980)
Saint Moritz, 1929
© ADAGP, Paris and DACS, London 2012/The Bridgeman Art Library
Medium: Oil on panel

André Edouard Marty (1882–1974)
An Evening at the White House, **advertisement for Cadillac Automobiles in** *Vogue,* **1929**
Medium: Colour lithograph

Tamara de Lempicka (1898–1980)
The Green Turban, 1929
© ADAGP, Paris and DACS, London 2012/The Bridgeman Art Library
Medium: Oil on canvas

Janet Clark
Summer Hat, c. 1930
© The Design Library, New York, USA/The Bridgeman Art Library
Medium: Watercolour on board

Janet Clark
Winter Fashion Design, c. 1930
© The Design Library, New York, USA/The Bridgeman Art Library
Medium: Watercolour on board

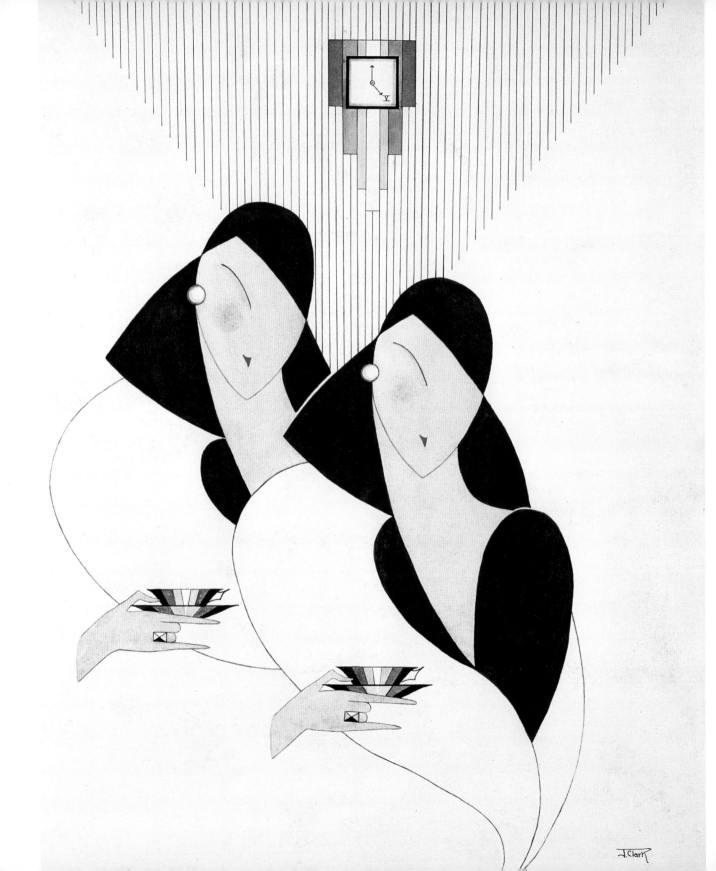

Janet Clark
Two Ladies Taking Tea, c. 1930
© The Design Library, New York, USA/The Bridgeman Art Library
Medium: Watercolour on board

André Edouard Marty (1882–1974)
The Picnic, **a London Transport poster,**
published by Underground Electric Railways Company Ltd, 1931
© ADAGP, Paris and DACS, London 2012/The Bridgeman Art Library
Medium: Colour lithograph

Erté (Romain de Tirtoff) (1892–1990)
Le Harem Moderne, **based on a costume design for** *Les 1001 Nuits,* **1927**
© Sevenarts Limited
Medium: Embossed serigraph

André Edouard Marty (1882–1974)
Canoeing, **a London Transport poster,**
published by Underground Electric Railways Company Ltd, 1931
© ADAGP, Paris and DACS, London 2012/The Bridgeman Art Library
Medium: Colour lithograph

Tamara de Lempicka (1898–1980)
The Orange Turban, **1935**
© ADAGP, Paris and DACS, London 2012/The Bridgeman Art Library
Medium: Oil on canvas

Erté (Romain de Tirtoff) (1892–1990)
Symphony in Black, based on an original design, 1938
© Sevenarts Limited
Medium: Serigraph

Index of Works

General Index